People eat
bread all over
the world.

7

There are many kinds, many shapes, many sizes—

ANN MORRIS

BREAD · BREAD · BREAD

PHOTOGRAPHS BY
KEN HEYMAN

HarperCollins*Publishers*

Bread, Bread, Bread
Text copyright © 1989 by Ann Morris
Photographs copyright © 1989 by Ken Heyman
Manufactured in China.
For information address HarperCollins Children's Books,
a division of HarperCollins Publishers,
195 Broadway, New York, NY 10007.

Library of Congress Cataloging-in-Publication Data
Morris, Ann.
  Bread, bread, bread.
    p.   cm.
  Summary: Celebrates the many different kinds of bread and how it may be enjoyed all over the
world.
  ISBN 0-688-06334-9 — ISBN 0-688-12275-2 (pbk.)
  1. Bread—Juvenile literature.   [1. Bread.]   I. Heyman, Ken, ill.   II. Title.
TX769.M664   1993   92-25547
641.8'15—dc20   CIP
                                                                                           AC

First paperback edition, 1993

Visit us on the World Wide Web!
www.harperchildrens.com

14 15 SCP 20 19 18 17 16 15 14

BREAD · BREAD · BREAD

skinny bread,

fat bread,

round flat bread,

bread with a hole,

9

crunchy bread,
lunchy bread…

10

and bread
to soak up
your egg.

11

Pizza, pretzel…they are bread too.

Bread on the table…

bread on your head.

Bread is good for you.

It helps
you grow.

It makes
you strong.

Making bread, shaping bread,

baking bread,

toasting bread,

20

cooking bread over the fire.

Fill up
the basket…

off to the market.

Bread for sale!

Breaking bread together…

Have a bite…
delicious!

INDEX

14 PORTUGAL: Hard rolls are an essential part of a splendid meal in an outdoor cafe.

15 SICILY: This girl is carrying bread baked in an old-fashioned oven to the village main square, where it will be sold.

16 GREECE: This bread maker obviously enjoys the taste of her own bread, made from hand-milled flour and baked in an outdoor village oven.

17 UNITED STATES: Rolls especially made to hold hot dogs help make a meal for this Los Angeles boy on his way to a baseball game.

18 UNITED STATES: Making bread includes measuring, kneading, rising, punching, shaping, and baking.

20 UNITED STATES: A modern toaster for sliced bread does the job quickly and evenly.

20 ITALY: Bread toasted outdoors at a Gypsy camp smells and tastes wonderful.

21 MEXICO: Tortillas are a thin, flat bread that is baked on an open griddle.

22 ECUADOR: The woman is carrying the bread she made that morning to the market, where she will sell it to the people in the village.

22 PERU: This bread, just dumped from its baking tray into a basket, may look messy, but it tastes very good.

23 ISRAEL: This man uses a bicycle cart to bring his bread to market.

24 ISRAEL: This large raised loaf made of whole grains with a hole in the middle is popular in the Middle East.

25 HONG KONG: Several of the breads in this Hong Kong shop have sweet fillings in them.

25 GUATEMALA: Though the mother baked the bread, everyone in the family gets involved in arranging the loaves for sale.

26 ISRAEL: A Tel Aviv family celebrate the Sabbath by breaking bread together. Prayers are said over the special bread, called challah, at the beginning of the Sabbath meal.

29 UNITED STATES: There's nothing like home-baked bread!

◆◆◆◆◆◆◆◆◆◆◆◆◆◆◆◆◆◆◆◆◆ ANN MORRIS ◆◆◆◆◆◆◆◆◆◆◆◆◆◆◆◆◆◆◆◆◆

has taught young children in both private and public New York City schools, and has also taught at Teachers College, Columbia University; New York University; and Bank Street College of Education. She left the teaching field to become editorial director of the Early Childhood Department of Scholastic, Inc., where she produced a number of award-winning films, filmstrips, and other audiovisual materials. She now devotes full time to writing and developing children's books. Among her recent titles are *Night Counting, Sleepy Sleepy,* and *Cuddle Up.*

◆◆◆◆◆◆◆◆◆◆◆◆◆◆◆◆◆◆◆◆◆ KEN HEYMAN ◆◆◆◆◆◆◆◆◆◆◆◆◆◆◆◆◆◆◆◆◆

is widely recognized as a foremost photojournalist. A student of Margaret Mead, he coauthored two books with her, *Family* and *World Enough.* His photographs have appeared in many other books, including *The Family of Children*, a book about childhood around the world, and *The World's Family.* His photographs in these books have earned him the reputation as one of the world's most sensitive interpreters of the human condition.